NEVER STOP
DREAMING

summersdale

NEVER STOP DREAMING

Copyright © Summersdale Publishers Ltd, 2016

Images © Shutterstock

Summersdale Publishers Ltd
46 West Street
Chichester
West Sussex
PO19 1RP
UK

www.summersdale.com

Printed and bound in the Czech Republic

ISBN: 978-1-78685-024-9

Substantial discounts on bulk quantities of Summersdale books are available to corporations, professional associations and other organisations. For details contact Nicky Douglas by telephone: +44 (0) 1243 756902, fax: +44 (0) 1243 786300 or email: nicky@summersdale.com.

To......................................

From..................................

Nothing happens unless first we dream.

CARL SANDBURG

If a little dreaming is dangerous, the cure for it is not to dream less but to dream more, to dream all the time.

MARCEL PROUST

AH, BUT A
MAN'S REACH
SHOULD EXCEED
HIS GRASP,
OR WHAT'S A
HEAVEN FOR?

Robert Browning

Keep your eyes on the stars and your feet on the ground.

THEODORE ROOSEVELT

Your mind is your
instrument. Learn to
be its master and
not its slave.

REMEZ SASSON

Every day brings a
chance for you to draw
in a breath, kick off your
shoes, and dance.

OPRAH WINFREY

Capture your dreams and your life becomes full. You can, because you think you can.

NIKITA KOLOFF

HOPE IS BEING
ABLE TO SEE THAT
THERE IS LIGHT
DESPITE ALL OF
THE DARKNESS.

Desmond Tutu

Live as if you were to die tomorrow. Learn as if you were to live for ever.

MAHATMA GANDHI

Nothing is impossible;
the word itself says
'I'm possible!'

AUDREY HEPBURN

DREAMING IS
JUST THINKING
WITH YOUR
HEART.

Don't be pushed by your problems. Be led by your dreams.

RALPH WALDO EMERSON

For my part I know
nothing with any
certainty, but the sight
of the stars makes
me dream.

VINCENT VAN GOGH

To accomplish great things, we must not only act, but also dream; not only plan but also believe.

ANATOLE FRANCE

If my mind can conceive it, if my heart can believe it, I know I can achieve it!

JESSE JACKSON

A SINGLE DREAM IS MORE POWERFUL THAN A THOUSAND REALITIES.

Nathaniel Hawthorne

Hope is a waking dream.

ARISTOTLE

Dreams are illustrations... from the book your soul is writing about you.

MARSHA NORMAN

EVERY GREAT
ACHIEVEMENT
WAS ONCE
A DREAM.

No matter where
you're from, your
dreams are valid.

LUPITA NYONG'O

I dream things that
never were; and I say,
'Why not?'

GEORGE BERNARD SHAW

No matter how much falls on us, we keep ploughing ahead. That's the only way to keep the roads clear.

GREG KINCAID

Every great dream
begins with a dreamer.

HARRIET TUBMAN

YOU DON'T HAVE
TO SEE THE
WHOLE STAIRCASE.
JUST TAKE THE
FIRST STEP.

Martin Luther King Jr

Whatever you can do, or dream you can, begin it. Boldness has genius and power and magic in it.

JOHANN WOLFGANG VON GOETHE

Whatever the mind of man can conceive and believe, it can achieve.

NAPOLEON HILL

DREAMS ARE THE TOUCHSTONES OF OUR CHARACTERS.

Henry David Thoreau

Never give up on a dream just because of the time it will take to accomplish it. The time will pass anyway.

EARL NIGHTINGALE

The greatest glory in
living lies not in never
falling, but in rising
every time we fall.

NELSON MANDELA

Do not be embarrassed
by your failures; learn
from them and
start again.

RICHARD BRANSON

Sail away from the safe harbour. Catch the trade winds in your sails. Explore. Dream. Discover.

H. JACKSON BROWN JR

TIME SPENT
DREAMING IS
NEVER WASTED.

Be in love with your life.
Every minute of it.

JACK KEROUAC

May you live every
day of your life.

JONATHAN SWIFT

DREAMS ARE TRUE WHILE THEY LAST. AND DO WE NOT LIVE IN DREAMS?

Alfred, Lord Tennyson

We are such stuff
As dreams are made
on, and our little life
Is rounded with a sleep.

WILLIAM SHAKESPEARE

Act as if what you
do makes a difference.
It does.

WILLIAM JAMES

You have to dream
before your dreams can
come true.

A. P. J. ABDUL KALAM

Life isn't about finding
yourself; it's about
creating yourself.

GEORGE BERNARD SHAW

YOUR SOUL IS
ALL THAT YOU
POSSESS. TAKE IT IN
HAND AND MAKE
SOMETHING OF IT!

Martin H. Fischer

If you find you're stronger than you thought, don't waste a moment being surprised by it – be motivated and stronger.

TERRI GUILLEMETS

Shoot for the moon.
Even if you miss, you'll
land among the stars.

NORMAN VINCENT PEALE

YOU GET A
BETTER VIEW
WITH YOUR
HEAD IN THE
CLOUDS.

Follow your dreams,
work hard, practise
and persevere.

SASHA COHEN

If you doubt yourself,
then indeed you stand
on shaky ground.

HENRIK IBSEN

The only thing that will
stop you from fulfilling
your dreams is you.

TOM BRADLEY

What you get by achieving your goals is not as important as what you become by achieving your goals.

ZIG ZIGLAR

PRAY THAT
SUCCESS WILL NOT
COME ANY FASTER
THAN YOU ARE
ABLE TO ENDURE IT.

Elbert Hubbard

Your victory is right around the corner. Never give up.

NICKI MINAJ

To live a creative life,
we must lose our fear of
being wrong.

JOSEPH CHILTON PEARCE

I BELIEVE IN WRITING YOUR OWN STORY.

Charlotte Eriksson

She stood in the storm,
and when the wind did
not blow her way, she
adjusted her sails.

ELIZABETH EDWARDS

The limits of the possible
can only be defined by
going beyond them into
the impossible.

ARTHUR C. CLARKE

A journey of a thousand
miles begins with a
single step.

LAO TZU

I have found that if you love life, life will love you back.

ARTHUR RUBINSTEIN

EVEN LITTLE
DREAMS ARE
WORTH PURSUING.

It's never too late...
to be whoever you
want to be.

ERIC ROTH

Never dull your shine for
somebody else.

TYRA BANKS

MAN IS A GENIUS WHEN HE IS DREAMING.

Akira Kurosawa

You must be the change you wish to see in the world.

MAHATMA GANDHI

If you can dream it,
you can do it.

TOM FITZGERALD

Our aspirations are
our possibilities.

SAMUEL JOHNSON

Everything that is done in the world is done by hope.

MARTIN LUTHER

DREAM YOUR
DREAMS BY NIGHT.
LIVE YOUR DREAMS
BY DAY.

I will always find a
way and a way will
always find me.

CHARLES F. GLASSMAN

When you come
to a roadblock,
take a detour.

MARY KAY ASH

WE ALWAYS
MAY BE WHAT
WE MIGHT
HAVE BEEN.

Adelaide Anne Procter

Dreams are more real than reality itself, they're closer to the self.

GAO XINGJIAN

Success is getting what
you want. Happiness is
wanting what you get.

DALE CARNEGIE

A dream is what makes
people love life even
when it is painful.

THEODORE ZELDIN

I love life.
I love life to death.

EMMANUELLE RIVA

SUCCESS IS A
SCIENCE: IF
YOU HAVE THE
CONDITIONS, YOU
GET THE RESULT.

Oscar Wilde

Occasionally ask,
'What is the connection
between what I want
most in life and anything
I plan to do today?'

ROBERT BRAULT

Jump into the middle of
things, get your hands
dirty, fall flat on your
face, and then reach
for the stars.

BEN STEIN

SEIZE THE DAY AND SEIZE YOUR DREAMS.

What we do flows
from who we are.

PAUL VITALE

Believe you can and
you're halfway there.

THEODORE ROOSEVELT

Don't live down
to expectations.
Go out there and do
something remarkable.

WENDY WASSERSTEIN

Never stop pedalling to power your dreams.

TERRI GUILLEMETS

THE ROUGHEST ROAD OFTEN LEADS TO THE TOP.

Christina Aguilera

Some people dream of
success... while others
wake up and work
hard at it.

ANONYMOUS

You have to be strong
and courageous and
know that you can do
anything you put
your mind to.

LEAH LABELLE

ALWAYS CARRY
YOUR KEYS IN
YOUR POCKET
AND YOUR
DREAMS IN
YOUR HEART.

Big shots are only little shots who keep shooting.

CHRISTOPHER MORLEY

Hope is not a dream but
a way of making dreams
become reality.

L. J. SUENENS

Goals are dreams
with deadlines.

DIANA SCHARF-HUNT

In order to carry
a positive action, we
must develop here a
positive vision.

DALAI LAMA

ALL GREAT
ACHIEVEMENTS
REQUIRE TIME.

Maya Angelou

Knowledge is limited.
Imagination encircles
the world.

ALBERT EINSTEIN

Wheresoever you go,
go with all your heart.

CONFUCIUS

MY CHILDHOOD
MAY BE OVER
BUT THAT
DOESN'T MEAN
PLAYTIME IS.

Ron Olson

It always seems
impossible until it's done.

NELSON MANDELA

If we all did the things
we are capable of
doing, we would literally
astound ourselves.

THOMAS EDISON

When patterns are broken,
new worlds emerge.

TULI KUPFERBERG

It is not the mountains we conquer, but ourselves.

EDMUND HILLARY

THE MOST EFFECTIVE WAY TO DO IT IS TO DO IT.

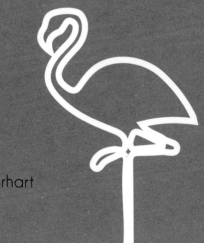

Amelia Earhart

Love the life you live,
live the life you love.

BOB MARLEY

Success comes from
knowing that you did
your best to become
the best that you are
capable of becoming.

JOHN WOODEN

YOU ARE
NEVER TOO
YOUNG OR
TOO OLD TO
ACHIEVE YOUR
DREAMS.

Do what you have to do
until you can do what
you want to do.

OPRAH WINFREY

Keep high aspirations,
moderate expectations,
and small needs.

WILLIAM HOWARD STEIN

If you take responsibility
for yourself you will
develop a hunger to
accomplish your dreams.

LES BROWN

One does not
discover new lands
without consenting to
lose sight of the shore
for a very long time.

ANDRÉ GIDE

TRUST YOURSELF.
YOU KNOW MORE
THAN YOU THINK
YOU DO.

Benjamin Spock

Laugh often,
dream big,
reach for the stars!

ANONYMOUS

Creativity is intelligence having fun.

ALBERT EINSTEIN

WHAT SEEMS
IMPOSSIBLE
IN REALITY
BECOMES
POSSIBLE WHEN
YOU DREAM.

We must never stop dreaming. Dreams provide nourishment for the soul, just as a meal does for the body.

PAULO COELHO

It takes a certain level of aspiration before one can take advantage of opportunities that are clearly offered.

MICHAEL HARRINGTON

All our dreams can come true, if we have the courage to pursue them.

WALT DISNEY

Commitment leads to action. Action brings your dreams closer.

MARCIA WIEDER

FAITH IS LOVE TAKING THE FORM OF ASPIRATION.

William Ellery Channing

With self-discipline, most anything is possible.

THEODORE ROOSEVELT

The man who moves a
mountain begins by
carrying away
small stones.

CONFUCIUS

LIFE IS VERY INTERESTING IF YOU MAKE MISTAKES.

Georges Carpentier

To succeed in life, you need three things: a wishbone, a backbone and a funny bone.

REBA McENTIRE

You are magnificent
beyond measure,
perfect in your
imperfections, and
wonderfully made.

ABIOLA ABRAMS

Once we believe in
ourselves, we can
risk curiosity, wonder,
spontaneous delight,
or any experience that
reveals the human spirit.

E. E. CUMMINGS

Rise above the
storm and you will
find the sunshine.

MARIO FERNÁNDEZ

HAVING A DREAM
IS THE FIRST STEP
TO MAKING IT
COME TRUE.

The way to develop
self-confidence is to
do the thing you fear
and get successful
experiences behind you.

WILLIAM JENNINGS BRYAN

Never look backwards
or you'll fall down
the stairs.

RUDYARD KIPLING

HITCH YOUR WAGON TO A STAR.

Ralph Waldo Emerson

Mix a little foolishness
with your serious plans.
It is lovely to be silly at
the right moment.

HORACE

Whenever you fall, pick something up.

OSWALD AVERY

Life is a great big canvas, and you should throw all the paint you can on it.

DANNY KAYE

A head full of dreams
has no space for fears.

ANONYMOUS

NURTURE YOUR
DREAMS AND THEY
WILL GROW TO
BECOME REALITY.

No one knows what he can do till he tries.

PUBLILIUS SYRUS

Find something you're
passionate about and
keep tremendously
interested in it.

JULIA CHILD

BE YOURSELF. THE WORLD WORSHIPS THE ORIGINAL.

Ingrid Bergman

To those who can dream,
there is no such place
as far away.

ANONYMOUS

The struggle you're in today is developing the strength you need for tomorrow. Don't give up.

ROBERT TEW

Reach high, for stars
lie hidden in your soul.
Dream deep, for every
dream precedes
the goal.

PAMELA VAULL STARR

There is no chance,
no destiny, no fate,
Can circumvent or
hinder or control
The firm resolve of
a determined soul.

ELLA WHEELER WILCOX

CREATIVITY
REQUIRES THE
COURAGE TO LET
GO OF CERTAINTIES.

Erich Fromm

In dreams and in
love there are
no impossibilities.

JÁNOS ARANY

My sun sets to
rise again.

ROBERT BROWNING

THE BEST DREAMS ARE THE CRAZIEST ONES.

If you don't build your own dream, somebody will hire you to help build theirs.

TONY A. GASKINS JR

All life is an experiment.
The more experiments
you make the better.

RALPH WALDO EMERSON

We become happier,
much happier, when
we realise life is an
opportunity rather than
an obligation.

MARY AUGUSTINE

Be brave enough to live creatively... what you discover will be wonderful. What you discover will be yourself.

ALAN ALDA

IT IS NOT IN THE
STARS TO HOLD
OUR DESTINY BUT
IN OURSELVES.

William Shakespeare

Trust in dreams, for in them is hidden the gate to eternity.

KAHLIL GIBRAN

The starting point of all achievement is desire.

NAPOLEON HILL

LIFE IS NOT ABOUT FINDING YOURSELF. LIFE IS ABOUT CREATING YOURSELF.

George Bernard Shaw

As soon as you start
to pursue a dream,
your life wakes up and
everything has meaning.

BARBARA SHER

Go after your dreams,
don't be afraid to push
the boundaries. And
laugh a lot — it's
good for you!

PAULA RADCLIFFE

What you do
today can improve
all your tomorrows.

RALPH MARSTON

If opportunity doesn't knock, build a door.

MILTON BERLE

YOU DESERVE TO
HAVE YOUR DREAMS
COME TRUE.

First say to yourself what you would be; and then do what you have to do.

EPICTETUS

The garden of the
world has no limits,
except in your mind.

RUMI

YOUR GREATEST
SELF HAS BEEN
WAITING YOUR
WHOLE LIFE:
DON'T MAKE
IT WAIT ANY
LONGER.

STEVE MARABOLI

You are never too old
to set another goal or
to dream a new dream.

C. S. LEWIS

If you're interested in finding out more about our books, find us on Facebook at Summersdale Publishers and follow us on Twitter at @Summersdale.

www.summersdale.com